This keepsake journal belongs to

_____ and _____.

It was started on

_____

(Date)

HOW TO USE THIS JOURNAL

To the moms out there-
This keepsake journal is designed to engage in spiritual discussions, boost confidence and open communication as you and your daughter get to know each other better. Before you start, your child needs to understand this journal is a "safe place" to open up and whatever she writes should not be criticized (poor grammar, spelling, handwriting, etc). You can use these topics as a springboard for deeper conversation. The journal is meant to help you bond. Start it with an open heart!

The journal includes a few mom/daughter challenges that will be beneficial to your relationship if you choose to complete them. Everything is optional- if your daughter doesn't want to draw or complete the coloring pages, she can skip it (although if she's not an artist, it could get a good laugh), but I encourage you to complete all you can.

Some kids are better at expressing themselves in written form. If your child is one of them, you may find writing to each other can be another source of communication you'd like to add regularly. At the end of the journal, there are blank pages if your daughter wants to share anything that is on her heart.This journal should be a fun project that you two can finish together. Through this process, your child will learn to be introspective as she analyzes and reflects on her own feelings. This skill will benefit her when she enters adulthood.

My process with back-and-forth journaling began in a blank journal with my daughters, currently ages 8 and 11. Because there were no prompts, we were free to write whatever we wanted, which ended up being a record of our daily activities. The entries lacked the depth and substance we are hoping to promote with this journal. My daughters provided input and insight as we developed a framework that we hope will encourage spiritual growth and habits. Each time we wrote, we left the journal on the other's pillow to be read as a nice surprise when we got into bed. Talk to your daughter and decide together on your preferred way to complete the journal. The last page contains a removable bookmark you can use to save your spot throughout the process. The next page includes preferences you can select together.

I truly hope this helps you and your daughter grow closer to each other and to God!

Happy Journaling!

Allison Sullins

> Moms and daughters, before you start, decide together how you'd like to complete it!

Questions to ask each other before beginning:

- Do we have to answer the pages in order? Yes or No
  (*If not answered in order, use the bookmark included on the back page to show where to start.*)

- Is it okay to skip the coloring pages? Yes or No

- Can I answer a few at a time? Yes or No

- Is everything shared confidential? Yes or No

- How long can we wait to respond? _____ days

- Where do we "deliver" the journal when we've finished our entry?

Other tips to consider:

- Is it okay if there are spelling errors? Yes! (This isn't English class!) If you need help understanding what to write or you want to ask for help with spelling, it's okay to ask your mom.

- What if you want to say/ask something that's not in the journal? There are some pages in the back that are open-ended for this reason (don't feel pressure to finish these if you don't need them).

- Remember to be honest and open in your responses!

- Grab some colorful pens and have fun with it!

THE JOY OF THE LORD IS MY STRENGTH.

Nehemiah 8:10

Just for fun!

What's Your Favorite?

DAUGHTER   **MOM**

COLOR

FOOD

MOVIE

HOLIDAY

BOOK

ANIMAL

BIBLE VERSE

TV SHOW

List 3 things you are grateful for no matter how small.

DAUGHTER

1.

2.

3.

MOM

1.

2.

3.

"Give thanks in all circumstances; for this is the will of God in Christ Jesus for you."
1 Thessalonians 5:18

DESCRIBE YOUR PERFECT DAY.

_____

_____

_____

_____

_____

_____

_____

MOM

MY PERFECT DAY WOULD BE...

_____

_____

_____

_____

_____

_____

_____

WHAT IS SOMETHING ABOUT YOURSELF YOU WOULD LIKE TO IMPROVE?

(Examples: being more organized, controlling your temper, being nice to your siblings, praying more, etc.)

DAUGHTER

_____

_____

_____

_____

MOM

_____

_____

_____

_____

I Thessalonians 4:1
"Excel still more"

DAUGHTER

TELL ME ABOUT YOUR FAVORITE VACATION OR FAMILY ACTIVITY. WHAT DID YOU LIKE BEST ABOUT IT?

MOM

TELL ME ABOUT YOUR FAVORITE VACATION. WHAT DID YOU LIKE BEST ABOUT IT?

DAUGHTER

Name 3 things you are good at ...

1. _____

_____

2. _____

_____

3. _____

_____

MOM

Name 3 things you are good at ...

1. _____

_____

2. _____

_____

3. _____

_____

WHO IS YOUR FAVORITE BIBLE CHARACTER? WHAT DO YOU LIKE ABOUT HIM/HER?

DAUGHTER

MOM

DRAW A PICTURE OF US DOING SOMETHING FUN TOGETHER.

DAUGHTER

DRAW A PICTURE OF US DOING SOMETHING FUN TOGETHER.

MOM

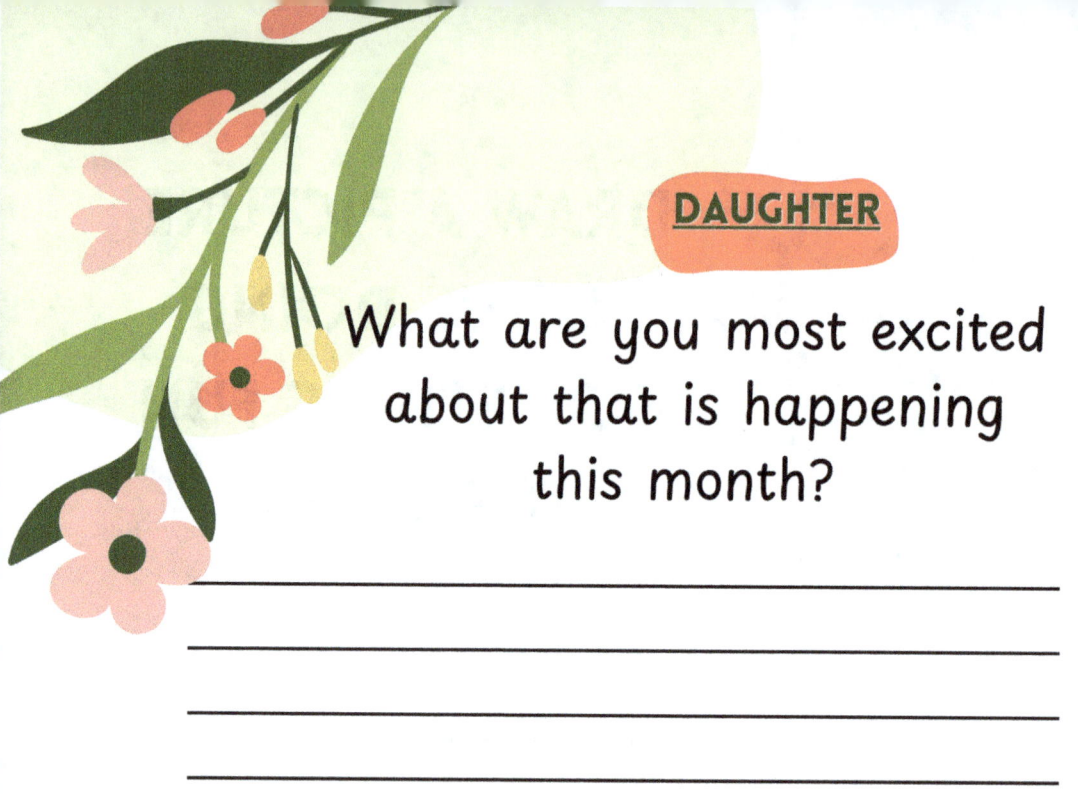

DAUGHTER

What are you most excited about that is happening this month?

_____

_____

_____

_____

MOM

What are you looking forward to?

_____

_____

_____

_____

_____

TRUST IN THE LORD WITH ALL YOUR HEART

PROVERBS 3:5

DAUGHTER
DO YOU WANT TO BE A MOM WHEN YOU GROW UP?
YES OR NO

HOW MANY KIDS WOULD YOU LIKE TO HAVE?
_____ GIRL(S)   AND _____ BOY(S)

DO YOU HAVE ANY NAMES ALREADY PICKED OUT?
IF SO, WHAT ARE THEY?

_____

_____

MOM
WHEN I WAS GROWING UP I ALWAYS
WANTED TO HAVE _____ KIDS
___ BOY(S) AND _____ GIRL(S)

Reasons I love my Mom

- _____
- _____
- _____
- _____
- _____

Reasons I love my daughter

- _____
- _____
- _____
- _____
- _____

GOD MADE A BEAUTIFUL WORLD! IF YOU COULD TRAVEL ANYWHERE IN THE WORLD, WHERE WOULD YOU GO?

Mom _____

_____

Daughter _____

_____

Genesis 1:31 "God saw all that He had made and it was very good."

"There will be showers of blessing."
Ezekiel 34:26

DAUGHTER:
NAME 5 BLESSINGS

1._____
2._____
3._____
4._____
5._____

MOM:
NAME 5 BLESSINGS

1._____
2._____
3._____
4._____
5._____

DAUGHTER

WHAT ARE SOME THINGS YOU WORRY ABOUT?

HOW CAN I PRAY FOR YOU THIS WEEK?

MOM

I'VE BEEN PRAYING ABOUT...

I Peter 5:7
"Casting all your anxieties on Him,
because He cares for you."

Worry Busters

- Pray to God about what's bothering you
- Read scriptures that encourage you (see below!)
- Take deep breaths
- Discuss it with an adult who can help you brainstorm solutions
- Do a calming activity such as drawing, coloring, journaling, painting
- Get active! Exercise can be a great stress reliever

John 14:1 "Do not let your hearts be troubled. You believe in God and also in me."

Luke 12:22 "Do not worry about your life, what you will eat, or your body, what you will wear."

Luke 12:24 "Consider the ravens: They do not sow or reap: they have no storeroom or barn, yet God feeds them. And how much more valuable you are than birds!"

Psalm 38:9 "O Lord, my desire is before You, my groaning is not hidden from you."

Psalm 94:19 "When anxiety overwhelms me, your consolation delights my soul."

John 14:27 "Peace I leave with you; my peace I give you. I do not give to you as the world gives. Do not let your hearts be troubled and do not be afraid."

INSIDE THE TROPHY DRAW OR WRITE SOME CHALLENGES OR WORRIES GOD HAS HELPED YOU OVERCOME!

<u>MOM</u>

John 16:33 "I have told you these things, so that in me you may have peace. But take heart! I have overcome the world."

Romans 8:37 "In all these things we are more than conquerors through Him who loved us."

INSIDE THE TROPHY DRAW OR WRITE SOME CHALLENGES OR WORRIES GOD HAS HELPED YOU OVERCOME!

DAUGHTER

John 16:33 "I have told you these things, so that in me you may have peace. But take heart! I have overcome the world."

Romans 8:37 "In all these things we are more than conquerors through Him who loved us."

Would You Rather?

DAUGHTER: CIRCLE YOUR CHOICE

MEXICAN FOOD OR ITALIAN FOOD

READ A BOOK OR WATCH A MOVIE

CHOCOLATE OR VANILLA

SLEEP IN LATE OR WAKE UP EARLY

BEACH OR MOUNTAINS

GO CAMPING OR STAY AT A HOTEL

SUMMER OR WINTER

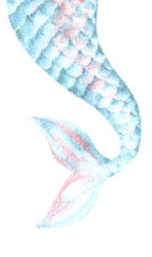

MERMAIDS OR UNICORNS

DOGS OR CATS

BE ABLE TO FLY OR BE INVISIBLE

BE AN AMAZING ATHLETE OR BE SUPER SMART

Would You Rather?

MOM: CIRCLE YOUR CHOICE

MEXICAN FOOD OR ITALIAN FOOD

READ A BOOK OR WATCH A MOVIE

CHOCOLATE OR VANILLA

SLEEP IN LATE OR WAKE UP EARLY

BEACH OR MOUNTAINS

GO CAMPING OR STAY AT A HOTEL

SUMMER OR WINTER

MERMAIDS OR UNICORNS

DOGS OR CATS

BE ABLE TO FLY OR BE INVISIBLE

BE AN AMAZING ATHLETE OR BE SUPER SMART

CAN YOU THINK OF A WAY TO BE MORE HELPFUL IN OUR HOUSEHOLD?

_____

_____

_____

_____

_____

_____

If you don't know right away, take a few days and look around! (If you still don't know, ask Dad if he's available☺)

Mom Challenge

PICK A NIGHT FOR ONE-ON-ONE TIME WITH YOUR DAUGHTER. IT DOESN'T HAVE TO INVOLVE SPENDING MONEY, JUST SETTING THE TIME ASIDE FOR THE TWO OF YOU. INCORPORATING 1:1 TIME CAN MAKE A CHILD FEEL SPECIAL AND VALUED.

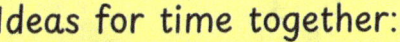

Ideas for time together:
- Baking
- Exercising
- Gardening
- Shopping
- Reading
- Neighborhood walks
- Sweet treats
- Board games

I Samuel 16:7 "For the Lord sees not as man sees; man looks on the outward appearance, but the LORD looks on the heart."

DAUGHTER

YOU MAY FIX YOUR HAIR OR PUT ON MAKE UP, BUT GOD CARES MORE WHAT YOU LOOK LIKE ON THE INSIDE. WHAT ARE SOME QUALITIES THAT MAKE YOU PRETTY ON THE INSIDE?

Circle the qualities that show inward beauty

Kind
Thoughtful
Nice hair
Joyful
Caring
Loving
Stylish clothes

Patient
Generous
Popular
Gentle
Slow to get mad
Pretty jewelry
Helpful

Put a star by the qualities that come more naturally to you and underline the ones you want to work on.

MOM

DO YOU HAVE ANY ADVICE FOR YOUR DAUGHTER REGARDING THIS TOPIC?

Draw a picture of our family

DAUGHTER

MOM

Growth

DAUGHTER

HOW MANY INCHES HAVE YOU GROWN THIS YEAR?

_____ INCHES

WHAT SIZE SHOE DO YOU WEAR? _____

Luke 2:52 "Jesus grew in both wisdom and in stature."

YOU'RE GROWING PHYSICALLY, BUT ARE YOU GROWING IN WISDOM?

_____

James 1:5 "If any of you lacks wisdom, let him ask God, who gives generously to all without reproach, and it will be given to him."

Challenge this week for Daughter and Mom:
- Read a Bible story (or chapter of the Bible) every night before bed.
- Pray together before bed and ask God to give you both wisdom.

Growth

MOM

SHARE A TIME WHEN YOU HAVE GROWN SPIRITUALLY OR SHARE SOMETHING YOU HAVE BEEN STUDYING/LEARNING ABOUT RECENTLY.

_____
_____
_____
_____
_____
_____
_____
_____

BONUS CHALLENGE:

READ THROUGH THE BOOK OF PROVERBS, ONE CHAPTER A DAY WITH YOUR DAUGHTER. THERE ARE 31 CHAPTERS SO YOU CAN START ANY DAY OF THE MONTH- COORDINATE THE CHAPTER WITH THE DATE (FOR EXAMPLE ON THE 5TH, READ CHAPTER 5).

Oh, how I love your law.
I meditate on it all day long.
Psalm 119:97

FUN MEMORIES WE'VE SHARED

DAUGHTER

1. _____
2. _____
3. _____
4. _____

DRAW ONE OF THE MEMORIES!

FUN MEMORIES WE'VE SHARED

<u>MOM</u>

1. _____
2. _____
3. _____
4. _____

DRAW ONE OF THE MEMORIES!

List a family tradition that you really like.

MOM

DAUGHTER

Do you have any traditions you would like our family to start?

MOM

DAUGHTER

Examples of Family Traditions
- Pizza and movie night every Friday
- Get ice cream after every first day of school
- Trip to the lake every Memorial Day
- Family devo every night before bed
- Create a Summer Bucket List together & complete it
- Paint pumpkins together on the first day of Fall
- Make fudge together at Christmas time

well done!

HAVE YOU DONE A FUN PROJECT FOR SCHOOL THAT YOU REALLY ENJOYED?

_____
_____
_____
_____
_____

WHAT'S YOUR FAVORITE SUBJECT?
_____

WHO HAS BEEN YOUR FAVORITE TEACHER?
_____

Ecclesiastes 9:10
"Whatever your hand finds to do, do
it with all your might."

<u>MOM</u>

WHAT WAS YOUR FAVORITE SUBJECT IN SCHOOL?

_____

DID YOU HAVE A PROJECT THAT YOU DID IN SCHOOL THAT STANDS OUT TO YOU?

_____

_____

WHO WAS YOUR FAVORITE TEACHER?

_____

Matthew 5:16
"Let your light shine before others, that they may see your good deeds and glorify your Father in heaven."

HOW DO YOU SHINE YOUR LIGHT?

MOM

Matthew 5:16
"Let your light shine before others, that they may see your good deeds and glorify your Father in heaven."

HOW DO YOU SHINE YOUR LIGHT?

DAUGHTER

DAUGHTER

WHAT'S YOUR FAVORITE BIRTHDAY MEMORY? _____

_____

_____

_____

IS THERE ANYTHING SPECIAL YOU'D LIKE TO DO FOR YOUR NEXT BIRTHDAY? _____

_____

_____

MOM

DO YOU HAVE ANY BIRTHDAY MEMORIES FROM YOUR CHILD-HOOD THAT STAND OUT?

_____

_____

_____

_____

_____

_____

DAUGHTER

What jobs do you think you would like to have when you grow up?

_____

_____

_____

MOM

DID YOU KNOW YOUR MOM ONCE WORKED AT....

_____

_____

_____

_____

_____

Jeremiah 29:11

"For I know the plans I have for you, declares the Lord, plans to prosper you and not to harm you, plans to give you a hope and a future."

The Bible is full of promises God has made.
What promises are you most grateful for?

MOM

DAUGHTER

Nehemiah 1:5
"LORD God of heaven, you are great and fearsome. And you
faithfully keep your promises to everyone who loves you
and obeys your commands."

God always keeps His promises!

LIST OF GOD'S PROMISES (THERE ARE MORE!)

- **THE RAINBOW IS A SIGN THAT GOD WILL NEVER DESTROY THE EARTH WITH WATER AGAIN (GENESIS 6:17)**
- **GOD'S PROMISES TO ABRAHAM (GENESIS 12)**
- **GOD GIVES US PEACE THAT PASSES UNDERSTANDING (PHILIPPIANS 4:7)**
- **GOD STRENGTHENS AND HELPS US (ISAIAH 41:10)**
- **GOD PROVIDES A WAY OUT OF TEMPTATION (1 CORINTHIANS 10:13)**
- **GOD COMFORTS US (ISAIAH 66:13)**
- **GOD NEVER FORGETS US (ISAIAH 49:15-16)**
- **ETERNAL LIFE (JOHN 3:16)**

WHAT IS SOMETHING THAT MAKES YOU LAUGH THE MOST?

Ha Ha Ha

WHAT IS SOMETHING YOUR DAUGHTER DOES THAT MAKES YOU LAUGH?

_____

_____

_____

_____

_____

_____

_____

_____

_____

_____

Proverbs 18:24
"A man who has friends must be himself
friendly. There is a friend who sticks
closer than a brother."

DAUGHTER

WHO ARE YOUR CLOSEST FRIENDS? _____

_____

WHAT ARE SOME TRAITS YOU LOOK FOR IN A GOOD FRIEND? _____

_____

IS THERE ANYONE YOU WISH YOU WERE CLOSER TO?

_____

DO YOU HAVE ANY FRIENDS YOU THINK YOU SHOULD SPEND LESS TIME WITH? IF SO, WHY? _____

_____

50

MOM

WHO WERE YOUR CLOSEST FRIENDS WHEN YOU WERE YOUR DAUGHTER'S AGE? _____

_____

_____

WHAT TRAITS DO YOU THINK ARE IMPORTANT TO HAVE IN ORDER TO BE A GOOD FRIEND?

_____

_____

_____

DO YOU HAVE ANY ADVICE ABOUT FRIENDSHIP?

_____

_____

_____

Friendship in the Bible
- David and Jonathan
- Daniel with Shadrach, Meshach, and Abednego
- Paul and Timothy
- Jesus and Lazarus
- Jesus with Peter, James, and John

IS THERE ANYTHING PERSONAL (EVEN EMBARRASSING) YOU'D LIKE TO ASK YOUR MOM ABOUT?

_____

_____

_____

_____

_____

_____

_____

_____

_____

_____

_____

_____

_____

_____

_____

_____

_____

_____

_____

_____

IS THERE ANYTHING YOU FOUND CONFUSING AS A KID THAT YOU WISHED SOMEONE EXPLAINED TO YOU BETTER?

_____

_____

_____

_____

_____

_____

_____

_____

_____

_____

_____

_____

_____

_____

_____

_____

_____

_____

_____

DAUGHTER

DO YOU LIKE TO SING? _____

ARE YOU INTERESTED IN LEARNING TO PLAY AN
INSTRUMENT? IF YES, WHICH ONE?_____

_____

WHAT'S YOUR FAVORITE SONG?_____

WHAT'S YOUR FAVORITE SONG FROM CHURCH?

_____

MOM

DO YOU LIKE TO SING? _____

DID YOU EVER LEARN TO PLAY AN INSTRUMENT AS A
CHILD? _____

WHAT'S YOUR FAVORITE SONG?_____

WHAT'S YOUR FAVORITE SONG FROM CHURCH?

_____

Sing to the Lord, for He has done glorious things.

Isaiah 12:5

In a world where you can be anything,

Be
Kind

DAUGHTER

DESCRIBE A TIME WHEN YOU SHOWED KINDNESS TO SOMEONE.

_____

_____

_____

_____

WHAT ARE SOME WAYS YOU CAN BE KIND TO OTHERS?

_____

_____

_____

Matthew 7:12
"Do to others as you would have them do to you."

WHAT ARE SOME WAYS AS A FAMILY WE CAN BE KIND TO OTHERS?

_____

_____

Daughter Challenge: If you have a sibling, do an act of kindness towards each sibling this week. (If you don't, choose someone else to be kind to.)

SPREAD *Kindness*

MOM

DESCRIBE A TIME WHEN YOU SHOWED KINDNESS TO SOMEONE.

_____

_____

_____

_____

WHAT ARE SOME WAYS YOU CAN BE KIND TO OTHERS?

_____

_____

_____

Ephesians 4:32
"Be kind to one another, forgiving each other, just as God in Christ has also forgiven you."

WHAT ARE SOME WAYS AS A FAMILY WE CAN BE KIND TO OTHERS?

_____

_____

Mom Challenge: Do an act of kindness this week to everyone in your immediate family.

57

DAUGHTER

WE WANT EVERYONE TO BE KIND, BUT UNFORTUNATELY NOT EVERYONE ACTS AS THEY SHOULD. HAVE YOU EVER HAD OTHER KIDS BE MEAN TO YOU OR SAY SOMETHING UNKIND? IF SO, DESCRIBE WHAT HAPPENED.

_____

_____

_____

_____

_____

If someone is unkind to you, you can say something like, "Friends don't let friends be mean to each other."

Stand up for yourself and stand up for other kids if you witness someone being unkind.

MOM

DO YOU HAVE ANY ADVICE FOR YOUR DAUGHTER WHEN SOMEONE IS UNKIND TO HER?

_____

_____

_____

Be kind to one another.

Ephesians 4:32

MOM

DESCRIBE SOME THINGS THAT WERE DIFFERENT WHEN YOU WERE A KID COMPARED TO NOW. DO YOU THINK LIFE WAS BETTER BACK THEN?

_____

_____

_____

_____

I WAS _____ YEARS OLD WHEN I GOT MY FIRST CELL PHONE.

DAUGHTER

WHAT DO YOU LIKE BETTER ABOUT NOW RATHER THAN WHEN MOM WAS A KID?

_____

_____

_____

_____

IS THERE ANYTHING THAT YOU THINK WAS BETTER BACK THEN?

_____

_____

_____

BIG EMOTIONS

WE ALL FEEL EMOTIONS. THAT IS NORMAL! OFTEN THEY ARE HAPPY ONES, BUT SOMETIMES THEY CAN FEEL STRONG AND IT CAN BE HARD TO KNOW HOW TO HANDLE THEM.

DAUGHTER

Circle any emotion you feel regularly:
Frustration Confusion Sadness
Anger Anxious Scared Disappointment

CAN YOU DESCRIBE TIMES WHEN YOU ARE FEELING THIS WAY?

_____
_____
_____
_____

TALKING ABOUT IT CAN HELP AND YOUR MOM IS ALWAYS WILLING TO LISTEN. HAVE YOU FOUND ANY TECHNIQUES THAT HELP YOU CALM DOWN?

_____
_____

MOM

WHEN YOU ARE FEELING A STRONG EMOTION, WHAT HELPS YOU STAY CALM?

_____
_____
_____

DAUGHTER

DO YOU HAVE ANY REWARDS OR ACCOMPLISHMENTS YOU ARE PROUD OF?

_____
_____
_____

CAN YOU THINK OF TIME WHEN YOUR MOM HAS MADE YOU FEEL SPECIAL? WHAT WAS IT? _____
_____
_____

MOM

DO YOU HAVE ANY AWARDS OR RECOGNITIONS YOU RECEIVED IN THE PAST? _____
_____
_____
_____

WHAT ARE SOME OF YOUR FAVORITE THINGS TO DO TOGETHER?

DAUGHTER

_____

_____

_____

_____

_____

MOM

_____

_____

_____

_____

_____

"I prayed for this child, and the Lord has granted me what I asked of Him."
1 Samuel 1:27

Describe the day your daugther was born. What did you think when you first saw her?

Why did you pick my name?

How does this makes you feel?

WHAT'S A WAY YOU HAVE GIVEN TO OTHERS?(CAN BE MONEY, TIME, OR ACT OF SERVICE)

_____

_____

_____

_____

_____

_____

_____

_____

_____

Acts 20:35
"It is more blessed to give than to receive."

WHAT'S A WAY YOU HAVE GIVEN TO OTHERS?(CAN BE MONEY, TIME, OR ACT OF SERVICE)

_____
_____
_____
_____
_____
_____
_____
_____

Hebrews 13:16
"And do not neglect to do good and to share with others, for with such sacrifices God is pleased."

WORDS, WORDS, WORDS

Ephesians 4:29
"Let no unwholesome word proceed from your mouth, but only such a word as is good for building up."

The Bible is full of verses that show us how we need to be careful what we say. Words are very powerful and we need to be mindful that they can be used for good or for bad.

WAYS WORDS CAN BE USED FOR A GOOD PURPOSE

- Honest words
- Kind words
- Give compliments
- Praise God with our words in songs or prayers
- Express thankfulness
- Build someone up
- Calm someone down
- Be polite

WAYS WORDS CAN BE USED FOR A BAD PURPOSE

- Lie
- Unkind words
- Call someone names
- Use "bad language"/curse words
- Gossip
- Tattle
- Yell at someone
- Complain
- Rude tone of voice

Proverbs 21:23
"Whoever keeps his mouth and his tongue keeps himself out of trouble."

LOOKING AT THE LIST WHERE WORDS CAN BE USED FOR A BAD PURPOSE, WHICH TWO DO YOU FIND THE MOST DIFFICULT TO FOLLOW?

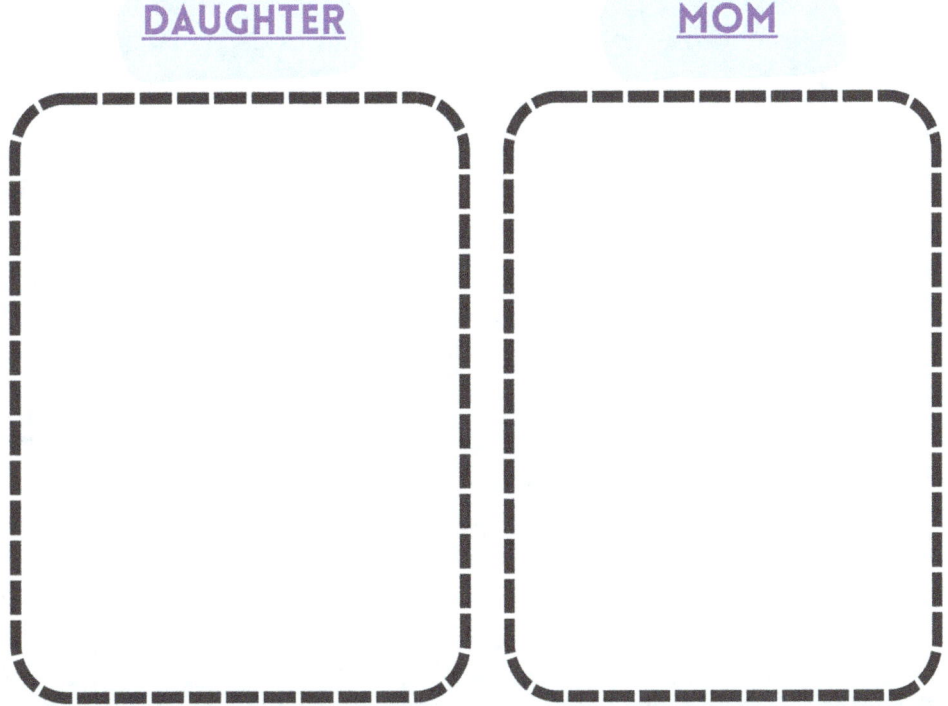

DAUGHTER

MOM

Focus this week on having kind, uplifting words!

I CAN DO

Hard

Things!

Colossians 3:23
"Work willingly at whatever you do, as
though you were working for the Lord
rather than for people."

MOM

WHAT IS SOMETHING YOU HAVE DONE THAT WAS HARD/CHALLENGING?

_____
_____
_____

HOW DID IT MAKE YOU FEEL TO COMPLETE THAT TASK?

_____
_____

DO YOU HAVE ADVICE OR ENCOURAGEMENT FOR YOUR DAUGHTER WHEN SHE HAS TO DO SOMETHING HARD?

_____
_____
_____

DAUGHTER

DESCRIBE A TIME WHEN YOU HAVE COMPLETED SOMETHING HARD/CHALLENGING.

_____
_____
_____

IS THERE SOMETHING YOU ARE UNSURE YOU CAN DO?

_____
_____
_____
_____

Philippians 4:13
"I can do all things through Christ who strengthens me."

DAUGHTER

DO YOU HAVE AN ACTIVITY OR HOBBY YOU WOULD LIKE TO LEARN?

_____

_____

SOME EXAMPLES:

- SEWING
- SPORTS
- PAINTING
- VOICE LESSONS

- PLAY AN INSTRUMENT
- TAE KWON DO
- COOKING
- KNITTING

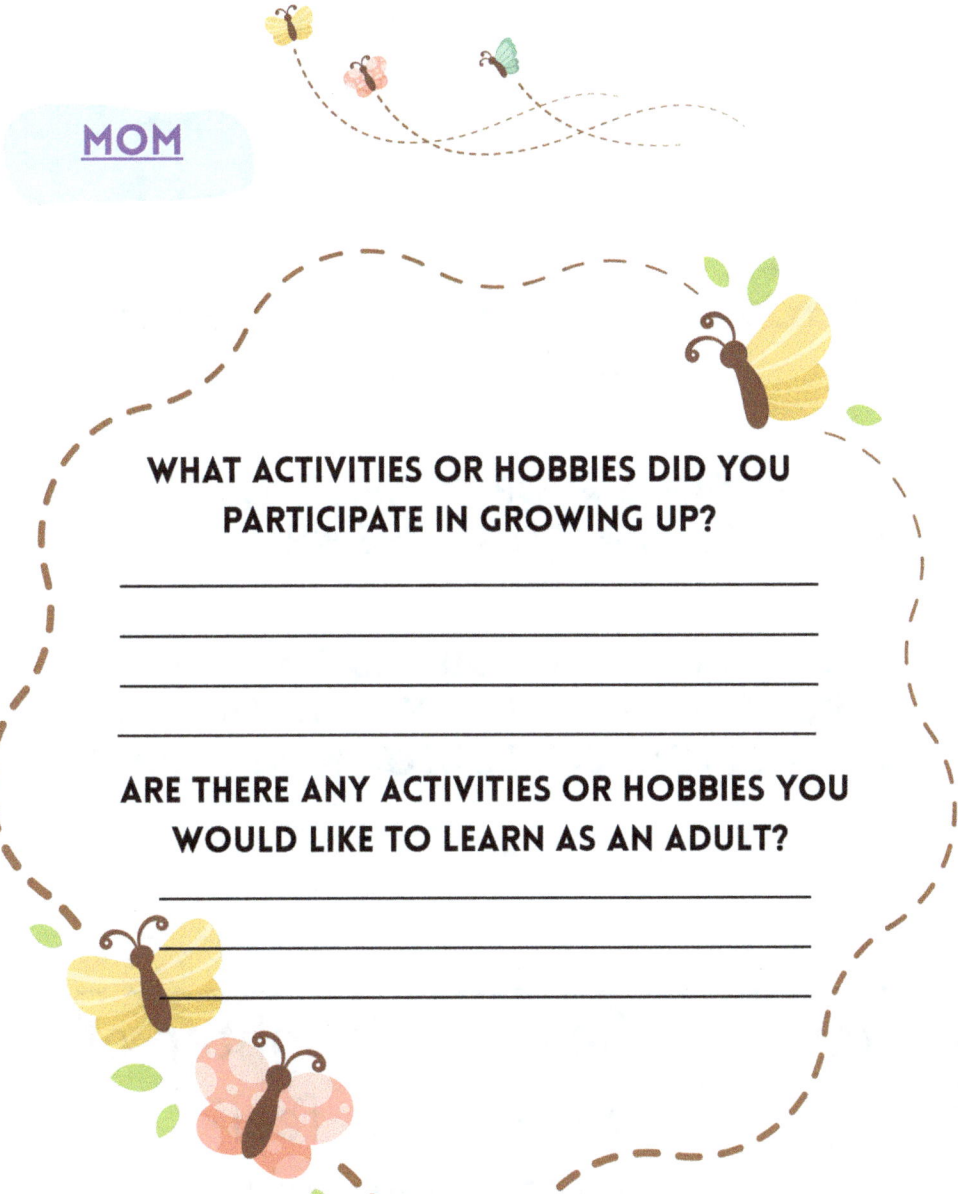

MOM

WHAT ACTIVITIES OR HOBBIES DID YOU PARTICIPATE IN GROWING UP?

_____
_____
_____
_____

ARE THERE ANY ACTIVITIES OR HOBBIES YOU WOULD LIKE TO LEARN AS AN ADULT?

_____
_____
_____

2 Corinthians 6:18
"I will be a Father to you, and you will be my sons and daughters says the Lord Almighty."

DAUGHTER

DID YOU KNOW YOU ARE A DAUGHTER OF THE KING? YES OR NO

YOU ARE GOD'S ADOPTED CHILD WHICH MEANS YOU ARE A PRINCESS OF THE WHOLE WORLD!

GOD CARES FOR YOU AND SEES YOU AS IMPORTANT. GOD GIVES YOU STRENGTH AND ABILITIES THAT CAN BE USED IN HIS KINGDOM.

How does being a daughter of a king make you feel?
(Circle all that apply to you!)
confident   happy   excited   hopeful
special   amazing   loved

<u>MOM</u>

Romans 8:16-17
"The Spirit himself bears witness with our spirit that we are children of God, and if children, then heirs- heirs of God and fellow heirs with Christ."

Proverbs 31:29
"There are many virtuous and capable women in the world, but you surpass them all."

DO YOU HAVE ANY THOUGHTS ABOUT BEING A DAUGHTER OF A KING?

_____

_____

_____

How does being a daughter of a king make you feel?
(Circle all that apply to you!)

confident   happy   excited   hopeful

special   amazing   loved

Draw a picture of yourself with a crown

MOM

DAUGHTER

Let all that you do, be done in love.
1 Corinthians 16:14

Name some prayers God has answered for you!

DAUGHTER

MOM

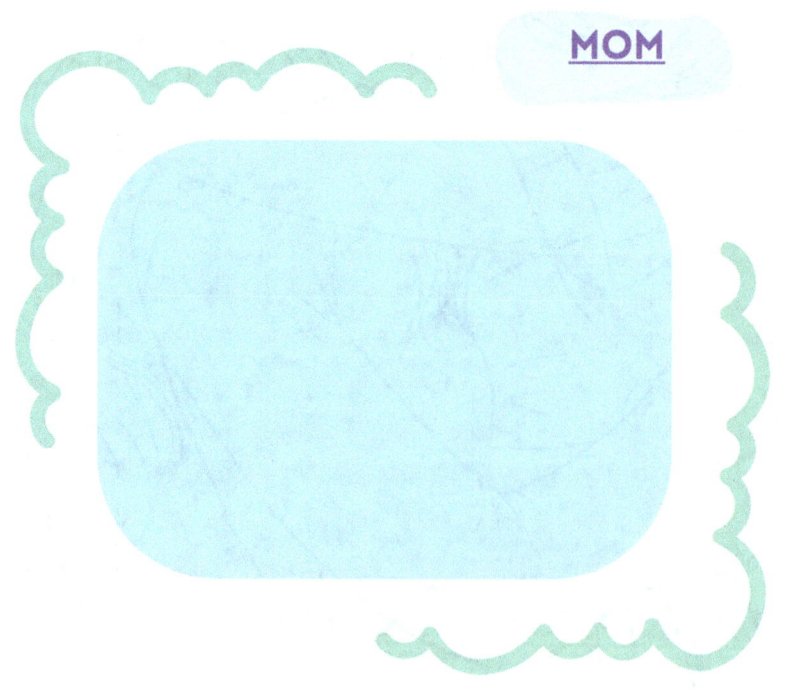

How
can I
pray
for you
this
week?

MOM

DO YOU LIKE TO COOK? _____

DO YOU ENJOY TRYING NEW FOODS? YES OR NO

WHAT ARE SOME OF YOUR FAVORITE MEALS YOUR MOM MAKES?

_____

_____

_____

IS THERE ANYTHING YOU'D LIKE TO LEARN HOW TO MAKE?

_____

_____

DO YOU HAVE ANY FAVORITE FOODS YOUR FAMILY EATS ON HOLIDAYS?

_____

_____

_____

_____

_____

_____

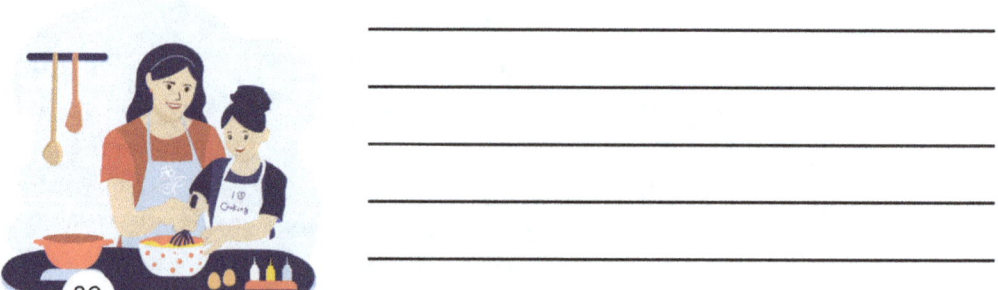

MOM

WHAT IS YOUR FAVORITE FOOD?

_____

DO YOU LIKE TO COOK?

_____

_____

DO YOU HAVE ANY SPECIAL FOODS THAT YOU MADE WITH YOUR MOM OR RELATIVE GROWING UP?

_____

_____

_____

DO YOU MAKE ANY FOODS DURING THE HOLIDAYS THAT YOU HAD WHEN YOU WERE GROWING UP?

_____

_____

_____

_____

Daughter Challenge:

Come up with 3 dinner ideas for this week!

1. _____
2. _____
3. _____

Mom Challenge:

Have your daughter help you cook one of the meals she chose!

Better is a dish of vegetables where love
is, than a fattened ox served with hatred.
Proverbs 15:17

DAUGHTER

DESCRIBE A TIME WHEN YOU FELT LOVED.

_____

_____

_____

WHO IN YOUR LIFE LOVES YOU?

_____

_____

HOW CAN YOU SHOW LOVE TO OTHERS?

_____

_____

Daughter Challenge:
Do something to show love to
your mom this week!

MOM

DESCRIBE A TIME WHEN YOU FELT LOVED BY YOUR DAUGHTER.

_____

_____

WHO IN YOUR LIFE LOVES YOU?

_____

HOW CAN YOU SHOW LOVE TO OTHERS?

_____

_____

Mom Challenge: Leave a note for your daughter on her bedroom door or in her lunch box every day this week describing something you love about her!

WHAT ARE 4 THINGS YOU LIKE ABOUT YOURSELF?

1._____

2._____

3._____

4._____

WHAT ARE 4 THINGS YOU LIKE ABOUT YOURSELF?

1._____

2._____

3._____

4._____

Acts 11:23
"When he (Barnabas) came and saw the grace of God he was glad and he exhorted them all to remain faithful to the Lord with steadfast purpose"

DAUGHTER

In the book of Acts, Barnabas is known as "the son of encouragement." Encouragement involves actively seeking opportunities to uplift and support others. You can start these habits even when you're young.

DESCRIBE A TIME WHEN SOMEONE CHEERED YOU UP AND ENCOURAGED YOU.

_____
_____
_____

_____

DESCRIBE A TIME WHEN YOU CHEERED SOMEONE UP!

_____
_____
_____

Examples of ways you can be an encourager too!
- Write or color a card for someone who is sick
- Find an older person at church to visit or talk to
- Invite someone to sit with you during lunch or at church
- Cheer on your friends/siblings when they do well
- Smile and talk to someone who looks like they are having a bad day

DESCRIBE A TIME WHEN SOMEONE CHEERED YOU UP AND ENCOURAGED YOU.

_____

_____

_____

_____

DESCRIBE A TIME WHEN YOU CHEERED SOMEONE UP!

_____

_____

_____

DOES ENCOURAGEMENT COME NATURALLY TO YOU?

_____

_____

_____

Mother and Daughter Challenge:
Find a way to encourage someone this
week and then discuss what you did!

Do you have any memorable dreams you'd like to share?

DAURGHTER

_____

_____

_____

_____

_____

_____

_____

_____

_____

_____

Do you have any memorable dreams you'd like to share?

MOM

_____

_____

_____

_____

_____

_____

_____

_____

_____

_____

IS THERE ANYTHING YOU'D LIKE TO TELL ME?

IS THERE ANYTHING YOU'D LIKE TO TELL ME?

_____

_____

_____

_____

_____

_____

_____

_____

_____

_____

_____

_____

_____

_____

_____

_____

_____

_____

_____

_____

_____

_____

IS THERE ANYTHING YOU'D LIKE TO TELL ME?

CONGRATS

We Did It!
We completed our journal on

_____

(Date)

Growing Together

MOM _____

DAUGHTER _____

Her children rise up
and call her blessed.

PROVERBS 31:28